# The Edification

# of Eve

ISBN: 0-578-46570-1

ISBN-13: 978-0-578-46570-8

*This book is dedicated to those who seek to know and truly love themselves. My prayer is that you find hope and guidance in every life lesson and remember that you are never stuck, you are only in transition.*

# CONTENTS

# ACKNOWLEDGMENTS

I want to say thank you to the Creator of my soul and my entire being. I am thankful for each lesson, even when I am unable to understand the pain or ambiguity of the situation. I trust you.

Also for my mother, who has also been my nurse, therapist, best friend, personal chef, muse, biggest fan, coach, and the heart of our family. I don't think that you will ever truly know how much you mean to me. I love you beyond words.

# Prelude [Preface]

Green, because nothing grows in the void of darkness.

When pupils are opened wide in anticipation it sees nothing and everything all at once.

The spill of red taints the joy that I attempt to feel.

Being cloaked in a bright radiant yellow would be a veil, hiding the blue-ish gray that I sometimes feel.

So in the wake of my rebirth, I chose green. A representation of renewal, growth, and serenity.

Green represents the changing of seasons from autumn to spring. It signifies that what was once dead is being brought back to life, and with that said, I humbly present to you the Edification of Eve.

**Note:** Peppered throughout this book there will be songs mentioned at the beginning of a poem. For me music is medicine, it's healing and offers reassurance that we are not alone in our pain. Any poem that includes the "Now playing" tag indicates that during the writing of that song, I found inspiration and comfort while listening to that song. For these instances, which aren't many, I recommend listening to the mentioned song while reading the poem.

# Learning: Vulnerability

Going through my divorce was one of the most challenging and painful experiences that I've ever had to endure. Divorce isn't always the answer, but for me it was redemptive. From the beginning things were seldom healthy or happy, yet still we were ordained by the Creator; but how can that be? Well, you see, out of the manipulation and verbal abuse that was pressed upon me came a seed that grew from the love that I had deep within me. Out of the pain came beauty, and that beauty was in the form of a child. How beautiful that even in pain can there be life and joy.

—and so really begins the breaking of old habits and familiarity to bring new love, pain, and ultimately edification.

## Best Parts

I give her the best parts of you.

Jazz tones, deep riffs and sultry melodies.

I tell her how intelligent she is as she quickly computes numbers together.
I say–
"You know that you get that from your dad, right?".

Yet I can't help but look grievously at the small patch of hair at the top of her spine,
That mirrors the one that you have.

And it's not that I miss you,
But more so that I'm still mourning the loss of everything that you were supposed to mean in my life,
–in our lives.

So like a tall tell that's passed through lineage from storyteller to storyteller,

I share with our daughter the beautiful stories of her father,

who still lives, –although our Marriage has died.

# Who, I am?

Now playing: Brown - [Roy Hargrove] & Vanguard [Jose James]

Oh how I would stretch from the high crown of my brown curly hair to the pointed tips of my toffee colored toes!

Limbs long and lanky, as if I were a giraffe, and with bones protruding from my skin, like a butterfly breaking from its cocoon.

I was always so wild and free −until I wasn't.

As time grew on me like kudzu vines, my inhibitions and child-like wonder was suffocated and turned into a homogeneous blanket of maturity and intellectualism.

I was as bland as the bowl of malt-o-meal that my mother would put before me at breakfast time.

I turned cold, then stiff as a board. Rigid and taste-less in my ways.

I was just like everyone else, and so I was accepted conditionally.

–Yet still, I did not accept myself.

And since that day I've been in ebbs and flows between wandering aimlessly and intently on my journey towards self discovery, trying to find out just exactly,

who, I am.

## Don't Think of Death

Don't think of death.

When you sit hopeless, know that there is triumph in your tears.

When you open your mouth to tell your story, know that there is fortitude in your words and strength in your struggle.

When you hope to God for release from this world,
because surely nothing hurts this bad, know that He will be the strength in your weakness and the endurance in your times of despair.

So cry if you must.
And scream if it's needed,
–But don't think of death.

## Energy Exchange

I sit hand in hand with you, and I'm not afraid to stare into your eyes.

People always said respect could be gathered in the gaze of one set of eyes set upon another, but I've never seen any truth in that.

The way I see it, total submission lies in the gaze of one's eyes upon another.

When I look into someone's eyes, it's always an exchange of energy,
as I open myself completely –unable to hold back any subdued thoughts or emotions.

It is within my stair, that I give up a piece of myself.

Vulnerable and unclothed in the bare white of my eyes,
–yes, it is only now that you see my soul.

17

It is only then that you see all of me,

complete in my vulnerability.

So although you may catch a glimpse of my eyes as they cross

paths with yours, know that only if they should stay is what

matters.

## First Love

You were the first to love me,

Although there were others before you.

You were gentle–

And remained faithful and loving.

So why is it now that we find ourselves broken?

Unable to piece back together our love.

Is it because we've fallen victim to circumstances beyond our
control?

My limited time?

Your limited mind?

No–

There are no victims here.

There are no victims when we both still have our words,

When we both still have our bodies,

When we both still have our ears to hear,

–to listen.

We stopped listening,

Although we heard each others tears.

We stopped talking,

Although our throats were swollen and full of things to say.

But then again,

Maybe they were just swollen shut.

Afraid of speaking out,

And sharing truths that could cut.

Afraid of expressing with words,

That had the potential to push us more a part than we already

were.

The truth stings,

but never more than the heartbreak of losing your first love.

## Expectations

It could've all been a dream,

For it only lasted for a moment in time.


How passionate we used to be.

How gentle our tone was.

How eager we both were to please.


But now it's as if neither one of us really cares.

Unwilling to fight, unwilling to bear,

–the distance that's grown in between us.


Like a boat leaving the shore,

–drifting farther and farther away.


We've drifted slowly,

But steadily a part.


Each of us so focused on ourselves instead of "us".

Now we're so far away that it doesn't even hurt as much to

say–

Goodbye.


Yet we still hurt,

–and we still cry.

## Process

Even though you and I are no more,
I refuse to delete our memories.

So I will not delete the pictures that I have of us—
Nor will I force myself to not think of you.

I will not avoid going to the places that we used to go to
together.

I will not erase your scent from my body,
—by forcing myself to get over you by sharing my body with
another.

No—
I will not drown out the remnants of your sweet voice in my
head with my own words of hurt and anger.

I will—
Remember you,

Because although I must grieve through this process–

I will always choose love above the pain.

## Virtually Lonely

We don't do things for the sake of doing them—
There's meaning behind even the most subtle of actions and
behavior.

Every move, every word, every action, every sentence—
Is an attempt to connect, to be understood.

Maybe this is the reason that an epidemic of souls feel lost,
disconnected, and alone.

We are seeking our connection through a digital barrier that
breaks down our words to flat meaningless text—
And our actions to displays of perfectionism.

Connected to millions all at once,
—yet to no single one person at all.

# *Learning: Patience*

After you've been through the pain of love and loss, and sometimes even while going through it, you begin to long for the happiness that you once felt. You long for not just that romantic love, but you long for a connection–not only to another, but also to yourself. You begin to wonder why haven't you been loving and cleaving to yourself as you have to other souls. You begin yearning to go through the healing process, you *want* to be a survivor and not a victim anymore. It's here in this space and place in life that you begin to learn one of the hardest of lessons–patience.

# I Wanted You

I wanted a home filled with your art,
–and your body spread across our bed.

I wanted your laughs to fill the room where we would sit and
enjoy quiet time together.

I wanted you.
All of you.
Every last piece,
–and every last inch.

Even the parts that I resented,
–I wanted.

Even the flaws that I cringed over,
–I wanted theml.

I promise you–
That I just wanted you.

## Exposure

Expose yourself to me in ways that you've never done before others.

Show me your soul–
Your pain,
Your highs,
Your lows.

Give me respect,
Devoted love,
Gentle words,
–and soft touches.

Fight for me like I'm all you've ever wanted,
Like I'm blood for your veins –and air to your lungs.

Come to me in humility,
With words that heal,
And hands to feel every pain that the others left behind.

Love me completely,
not just when it's convenient.
Please.
Love all of me,
or you'll have none of me at all.

## Free

I would love to end this poem with a slight bit of hope, but in all honesty I am still grappling with the high set expectations that oftentimes leave me high-strung in anxiety and in anticipation.

So with that I present to you just my thoughts.
I hope that even without a glimmer of possible hope in these lines, that you can at least find the time to at least try to understand.

———

How can I just be?

And do all of the things that I enjoy so passionately–
With no expectations of financial gain,
– or having the validation of someone knowing my name?

How can I set aside the self inflicted expectation of being all knowing while simultaneously maintaining sage-like peace?

When even I know that the idealism of possessing that type of perfection is completely un-idyllic.

How can I set free expectations of quantitative measures,

–that urge me to have more and to be more,
Important.

How can I release these qualitative desires that crave
validation and to feel that I am,
Enough.

I'm not asking for a solution because I understand that the
issue stems from lessons inbred since elementary.
It's that same oppressive system that use to enslave our bodies,
– but that now lock us up mentally.

And really all I'm wondering is–
How can I just be,
Free.

## Ethereal

Thoughts of a higher existence and a spiritual sign,
–craving for not just a warm body,
But an ethereal soul to share my mind.

## Some-One

Behind this smile and gentle attitude I yearn for authentic exchanges instead of friendly platitudes.

For a soul who asks, "how are you doing?", as a question rather than a statement.

Someone who has curiosity for my soul, instead of criticism for my mind.

Someone who just gets it.
Someone who gets, me.

Someone that pours into me pure love, consistently and genuinely. Someone whom I trust fully without inhibitions.

Someone–

Like me?

## Resurrection

Now playing: Vibin out with (((o))) [FKJ]

Souls longing for something gentle,
–someone who'll understand and know just how to love.

Slowly, with tenderness.
Patiently, with understanding.
Passionately, with adoration.

Feigning for the connection, that will bring my metaphysical
heart to a resurrection.

## Static Motion

I am a ball of static motion,
–tiny small pieces moving quickly and swiftly from here to there,
Forming thoughts and generating new ideas–

They come together in static motion to create every part of me.

They gather in my mind,
And in the tips of my fingers–
And then explode into words written on a sheet of paper.

They give me a feeling of being in motion even while I sit in the stillness of the morning.

With feelings of anxiousness,
I sit calmly and quietly waiting for them to move me to where I should be,
–like an anchored ship afloat in the middle of the ocean,

Here I am,
–as I sit in static motion.

## 30 Minute Dreaming

I sat outside peering up between the thinned out branches of infant trees and thought...

Wouldn't it be nice to always have moments like this?

Watching the clouds move with the time, looking up at the sun, getting golden brown as I sit, hearing the muffled voices of passerbyers?

Wouldn't it be nice to not have to clock in and out of happiness, in and out of life,
–in and out of my dreams?

Wouldn't it be nice.

## Jazz Epiphany

Now playing: A series of jazz songs [way too many to list]

Why is loving myself the hardest thing that I've ever had to do?

Had–to–do?

So much agony for something that I should freely just want to.

Giving to others always the benefit of the doubt, while inside of my head all I do is scream, fuss, and shout.

I am my worst enemy, but why?

# Who, I am?

Now playing: Brown [Roy Hargrove] & Vanguard [Jose James]

Oh how I would stretch from the high crown of my brown curly hair to the pointed tips of my toffee colored toes!

Limbs long and lanky, as if I were a giraffe, and with bones protruding from my skin, like a butterfly breaking from its cocoon.

I was always so wild and free –until I wasn't.

As time grew on me like kudzu vines, my inhibitions and child-like wonder was suffocated and turned into a homogeneous blanket of maturity and intellectualism.

I was as bland as the bowl of malt-o-meal that my mother would put before me at breakfast time.

I turned cold, then as stiff as a board. Rigid and taste-less in my ways.

I was just like everyone else, and so I was accepted conditionally. Yet still, I did not accept myself.

And since that day I've been in ebbs and flows between wandering aimlessly and intently on my journey towards self discovery, trying to find out just exactly who, I am.

# *Learning: Truth*

To think that I ever could hate you and be in a place of such pain and anger that I sought to escape completely from your love. Funny thing is that, all of my pulling away from you and anger towards you was in vain, because how could I ever be distant from your love, when you and I are one?

Psalms 139

7 Where can I go to hide from Your Spirit?
Where can I flee from Your presence?
8 If I ascend into heaven, You are there;
If I make my bed down below, behold You are there.
9 If I take the wings of the morning,
And dwell in the uttermost parts of the sea,
10 Even there Your hand shall lead me,
And Your right hand shall hold me.
11 If I say, "Surely the darkness shall fall on me,"
Even the night shall be light about me;
12 Even the darkness cannot hide from You,
Because the night shines as the day with You;
Yes, the darkness and the light are both alike to You.

# Blooming

I am a flower blossoming into a thousand suns–
A flower that bloomed so beautifully, but then withered and
died once the cold harsh winds of autumn came.

And just when you began to believe that nothing could ever
be eternal and last forever,
Spring came again and revealed to you that I was in fact a
perennial–

Cycling from earth to ashes,
And from death back into life–
For all of eternity.

## Believe

I will believe in your goodness,
–even though I cannot see.

I will sing of your peace, and of your mercy,
–because you loved me before my very existence.

You watch over me,
While I lay in doubt.

You love me,
While I am still in my wretched ways.

You restore my strength,
–and listen to my cries when no one else cares.

You lift me up and give me hope,
In the midst of my afflictions.

You are the freedom from pain that I seek,
You are the sunlight that seeps into my soul and fills me with joy.

Selah.
Amen.
All glory be to the One that is,

and was–
And is yet to come.

## Light

God takes me as I am and pours into me new vision and new desires.

I look to Him to remove my fleshly doubts and desires,
–and to create in me a new creature.

I medicate myself with His word,
And with the words of wisdom from many books that came after.

I fill my lungs with praise and adoration.

I exhale the negativity of hatred, jealousy, and fear.

These are not me,
–and not who He's created me to be.
For the holy book says,

*"God has not given us the spirit of fear, but of love, patience, and a sound mind"*

So I release all those worldly things,
–and fight to hold onto what is just, what is His light, and what heals me from the inside out.

## Only Humanity

Living in this brown skin has tinted my rose colored lenses from a cheerful rosey pink into a gray dreary smut.

Always viewing the world from the perspective of an outlier, an outsider, looking in.

Seeing black and white, only because it had been made clear to me from the very beginning that my blackness is different.

That it is lesser, more volatile, and singed in suffering.

Oh, but what they fail to see is that humanity came from blackness, from nothingness.

It is only our humanity that ties us each together, to create the joy that we seek.

Truly, what is missing in yourself can be found in the differences in others, for we are made in His likeness, and in His image we are all made equal.

One in the same, but still unfamiliar in ways that we must be intentional in learning to love.

## Mini gods

People have so much to say.

They breakdown situations and circumstances making sense out of ambiguity,
In a tasteless attempt to control what they don't understand.

But what they can't understand is that somethings are metaphysical, ethereal, and unable to be logically explained.

Some things are undeniably Godly.
Indescribable
Unimaginable
Unfathomable

Yet man[y] will unbind, unwind, and undermine what is meant for the almighty.

We will tell of truths and of God's divine thoughts and wisdom, as if we transcribed his word ourselves.

As if we truly know Him,
When we don't even know ourselves.

We judge,
then we forecast others fate.

45

But who amongst you can cast words of discrimination?
When you lack faith,
You lack love
You lack mercy
You lack forgiveness
You lack compassion.

Do you not know that you are merely a vessel?
Meant to carry His love, and not your own hatred and languishing hope of the human race?

You are His,
−and his alone.

You are not your own,
so stop speaking with words to serve yourself and your supposed beliefs.

Your beliefs should be your actions, and your actions should draw others to Him.

And if that is not your mission, then mute your ramblings and open your heart to Him to breathe into you,

Hope
Love
Truth

And compassion.

## More

I noticed that the more I ventured out,
The more clarity I received in my soul that my life was
destined for something greater,
Something lighter–
But more.

Not more in terms of quantity,
–but more in terms of substance.

More depth.
More love.
More forgiveness.
More joy.
More of everything that I had been denying my soul,
–and less so what I currently held presently as my reality.

## Nobody's Savior

But wait...

I have more to say–

I am nobody's savior.

I can't fix you,
Or heal your pain,
–although I've tried so many times before.

I'm not your everything.
I'm not your strength,
–or your peace.

I am not your saving grace,
–or your happiness...
Especially when sometimes I find it difficult to carry that same joy, that I share.

I am not the perfection that you've made me to be,
I am only me.

I am just as imperfect and human as you are.
So please believe me when I say that I cannot save,
–nor heal you.

And although I pray for you,
From early morning into the late hours of the evening,
And until my knees have been scraped and bruised,

I have to remember that even in my doing–
And even in the depths of my compassion and empathy,
–I am nobody's savior.

# *Learning: To Let Go &*

# *Heal*

It's a conundrum how we as humans seek constantly for gratification. For joy and peace, yet we torment ourselves with negative self talk and with yearning to be anything other than ourselves. I have to confess that this is still a lesson that I am learning, to let go and to heal. I feel as souls taking residence in our physical forms, we are in a constant battle of accepting ourselves as a physical being and accepting who/what we truly are, which is an ethereal being. We truly aren't the bodies that we take as our homes. We are souls of substance that beg to be heard and acknowledged through the physical shells that we call our bodies. It is certain that we will hit highs and lows—and we will ebb and flow for the eternity that will ultimately end when our bodies fail us and it is our time to return to our true selves.

## Fate

Such a harsh word to call destiny.

When another being's free will can take over my own, and become misery.
How can we call that destiny?

If what will be will be,
Why give me a false sense of identity?

A false sense of well-being,
That everything will be alright in the end.

Oh? But will it?

Can you look into my eyes and tell me my future?
Can you read the creases of my palms, or the astrological meaning of my sign and tell me for sure what will become of me?

If karma will come and repay my deeds,
And if I will reap what I have sown,
–then how can there be fate?

How can there be a series of unfortunate,
or I would hope–

Fortunate events that serendipitously befall me without any explanation?

This is why I sigh deeply when I hear someone utter the word fate.

Mmm, such a harsh word to call destiny.

# Tired

I'm tired of being a product of the opinions of others—

My words misinterpreted as harmful when good intent was all I ever meant to express.

And my facial expressions,
—while in deep thought being assumed as a suggestion of personal detest.

Because according to those who live outside of my body—
I'm too loud when I laugh,
—or when I make an attempt to express myself.

And when I'm direct it's looked upon as disrespect.

I feel forced to smile every time I pass a stranger,
So that my stoic nature isn't distorted as anger.

I feel weary and self loathing—
With so many faces and spaces pushing and pulling.

Categorizing me under their specified definitions,
While placing their acceptance of me under their,
—"is she qualified" conditions.

My hair deemed unprofessional.
My skin seen as extraterrestrial.

My nationality seems American,
–but my ethnicity is a mixture of African royalty and the native people who now reside on reservations that used to be sacred land.

For the life within me I just can't seem to understand–
...why?

Why fear what you refuse to comprehend?

And you'd rather destroy me than to put away your hate and distaste for what could be a friend.

I wonder, I ponder, I think, I toss and turn over this daily.

Each day rising,
–still with no resolution to this injustice,
And quite frankly I'm just tired.

But–
I Still Love You

Why do I want to remember you?

A lover who couldn't love me the way that I needed to blossom,
– yet you brought me back to life when I was closer to death than cold breath and icy fingertips.

You reeled me in with the promises of love,
A nostalgic tonic of–
1 part mystery,
2 parts unrequited love,
– and an overdose of ego and obscurity.

Unwilling to let your veil fall so that I could see you for who you really were, you hid behind a collection of ideals and platitudes,
– misrepresented as perfection.

I begged and pleaded to know just who you were in raw form,
But you just didn't have a clue that all that I really wanted–
Was to know you.

## I Don't Cry Anymore

I don't cry anymore
I just write the pain away.

Each letter is a tear,
Falling onto the paper.

Soaking through the sheets
Scattering this way, and that way, and over into subsequent sheets,

Reminding me that there's something that I want to say–

That I've GOT to say.

That I'm hurting.
And that I feel like I'm dying inside.

An externally emotionless being,
that is bleeding from the inside out.

Crying through the words left on each sheet
The ink is the pain that runs out with each word.

Until the ink runs dry–
Because I've cried too much and I've written enough.

## Brainwashed

In my mind I have so much to say. The words surround my cerebral cortex and tighten themselves around my nerves endings.

I breathe in, I breathe out.

My chest extends then collapses when I open my mouth and begin to speak. It's as if all of my words have left me and my thoughts have become mere ghost in the cemetery that I call my mind.

I try to steady my hands from shaking, I try to steady my voice from trembling, but it's as if I have no control over my own body.

To others I look ill prepared and aloof, but deep within the realms of my inner workings I am ashamed and afraid.
–and unable to speak.

I feel ignorant and unworthy as I sit beside those who are self assured and confident.
–seemingly.

And still my mind yells out to me that there is no place for me here, and that I don't belong.

## The Time Just Fades

The time just fades–

Melting away like the sweet smelling wax of a burning candle
in the night.

A lingering memory that burns until it's gone.

Alienation that once stung without mercy,
–now wanes into a dim flicker.

And telephone calls quickly go from,
"How have you been"–
To meaningless bicker.

You tear me apart while I sit wondering why,
–you used to comfort my tears,
But now all you do is make me cry.

Even through all of the pain,
–I admit honestly,
I just really miss her.

And I'd give anything–
If I could just have my sister.

# Rain

A delicate drip,
–so subtle,
That it's hardly seen in the dimly lit night's sky.

Falling harder and more consistently,
Creating small gatherings of water on the ground.

Steady pouring,
–in abundance,
Flowing and settling in the crevices on a rooftop.

Slipping down the shingles,
Funneling down the gutters and back into the Earth.

Renewal.
Shedding of all that was,
–and becoming cleansed and ready for all that is to come.

## One Love

Now playing: I wish [Russell Gunn]

When I first laid eyes on you, I knew that I loved you.

You were so intentional, so self assured, so direct, so everything that I wasn't but wanted to be.

I gave up everything that I held close to me to spend time with you. I held within myself mistruths and uncertainty, never knowing if the feelings that I felt were virtuous.

I had been told so many times that loving you was something of a sin, but how can I begin to tell you how you saved me with the very essence of your tone,
–and your touch brought my entire soul back to life.

For that I will forever be grateful and will never forget the one love that you gave to me when no one else would.
–even until the end.

## Goodnight

Say goodnight to your anxious thoughts–

Say goodnight to the fears you have for tomorrow...

Say goodnight to the heartbreak,
–and the wondering...

Say goodnight as you close your eyes,
And open your mind to lucidly serene dreams–

Goodnight.

# Healing

Now playing: Healing Music of the Ocean [George Winter]

Transforming, a metamorphosis of the spirit...

Souls transcending–
Blending, shapeshifting and becoming anew.

The pouring out of all things that are impure and that do not
serve a bigger and greater purpose.

A cleansing of all hurt and pain from the center of your
physical being,
–to the very ends of your outer extremities.

New truths taking hold and creating something ethereal–

... Something rare,
–and something spiritual.

Stillness.
In the inner workings of your being you hear a whisper...

It is time.

# *Learning: What Love is*

Now playing: Infant Eyes (2002 - Remastered) [Wayne Shorter]

And now we arrive at the root of what I believe to be the inception of all of the things that we desire, both carnal and ethereal–Love. Love is something that a great number of us spend our entire lives searching for. We desire to give love and we desire even more so to receive love. The baffling thing is that no one teaches us really, how to love. There is no subject taught in school that educates young minds on how to genuinely and completely love themselves. And not with the ego, but with purity and humility. So we are forced to grow as unkempt wild vines until we ourselves decide to take the time to prune the parts of ourselves that have lain dormant and unquestioned. We must question our indoctrination of love. We must reform the question of, "what is love?" into a statement of, "what love is", because truly what we've been seeking has been within and all around us since our very own inception–

And that is, love.

## The Edification of Eve

It took a decade to figure out that he wasn't what my soul
needed.

Because you see,
he was built for my body, but not for my mind.

—or my spirit for that matter.

He was the selfish type,
but then again so was I.

I was looking for him to love me, respect me, treat me with
the love that I didn't even set aside for myself.

I was so blind to seeing the truth, and entirely deaf to
hearing what he was actually saying to me with every action.

I
    Don't
        Love
            You.

Why is that so hard to accept?

When his words said it to me every night when I would
allow him sanctuary in my body only to be dismissed as he
would rise up immediately after to leave my side.

No sweet scented words, or soft touches to tell me that my
body pleased him,
Just dismissal that I even existed.

But how can I possibly be angry with him?
–When it was me, who first dismissed myself.

My thoughts,
My self respect,
My morals,
My entire being.

I did this to me.

But now as I unlearn and relearn how to love,
I edify myself by placing me as a being deserving of my love
and respect.

No longer willing to be dismissed or denied what I am
deserving of,

And so I began the edification of Eve.

## Favorite Thing

It wasn't until I let go of everything,
–and everyone that lied externally,
That I began to realize that I could be enough,
All by myself.

I began to dance with joy,
–filled with so much love and appreciation for someone that
I had forgotten.

For a woman so deserving of adoration and respect–
Me.

I am my favorite thing.

## Being

I want more than anything else to be drenched in everything that is expressed through the soul.

I want my thoughts to paint in slow soft brush strokes.

I want my breath to breathe out richly pigmented colors of compassion, strength, courage, and love.

I want my steps to be steady and rhythmic,
–like a soulful jazz song.

I want my tears to flow like a twelve bar blues progression falling into a deep bellowing riff.

I walk by your pieces and can think of nothing else,
–but wanting to be consumed by every last oil and pastel color.

I long to melt into your subconscious,
–becoming one with you and being released onto your raw stretched canvas.

I want to blend into the rich colors that you dab onto your paintbrushes and expel onto the canvas as self expression.

I want to be your passion.
Your muse,
–your one great love.

Is it ok if I can just be?

Fervent Love

We'll let another weekend go by without contact, without so much as an,
"I love you" or " I'm thinking about you".

No amount of pride could keep apart two bodies who are truly, deeply, passionately, and completely in love.

I say to leave.
–and you leave.

Then there is silence.

We don't exist to love each other,
We exist to persist to fall in and out of each other's lives.

We argue pointlessly,
Until we miss each other and it hurts.

But still we don't heal the pain that either of us feel.
We'd rather starve to death of love than to heal effortlessly in the comfort of each other's arms.

And that's just why we won't work.
–because we refuse to fight passionately,

Intensely.
Tirelessly.

We refuse to go to war,
–because we're both already at war with ourselves.

And there's no way to make up for what I need from you,
Because either we have it or we don't.

The truth of the matter is that being truly in love means being
each others antidote.

So ask yourself this...
are we each other's cure or toxin?
–and am I your good luck charm,
Or your kryptonite?

## Common Love Don't Suit Me

Common love don't suit me
I want a love that burns
One that ignites like propane and fire
One that leaves a scorch that can't be scrubbed off
I want a love that makes the world spin
And where time escapes,
–being loss like tiny grains of sand slipping through your fingers
I want a love that sweeps me from off of my feet
Never the same, yet always consistent
Willing to compromise,
–one that isn't resistant
Because common regular old love just doesn't suit me
It has to be bold
Assuring, unfaltering, forgiving
It has to unfold me, mold me, and hold me
In those times when I'm feeling unsure
It has to lead me, feed me, and not impede me
It has to be that Corinthians kind of love that is both patient and kind
The kind of love that I can truly call mine
Because common love doesn't suit me.

## The Price of Love

Someone once told me that no love here on Earth is
unconditional.

It all comes with a price.
So what's your price?

Is it attention?
Loyalty,
– or respect?


Words of adoration and love?
–Or maybe all of the above?

## Consummation

You were never horrible towards me,
But you were never really good to me either.

You took a fragile frame already broken down and bruised,
And reached inside to take any goods that remained.

You didn't abuse me like he did,
But you used me until I had no more left to give.

And the only reason that you stayed,
–was for my weaknesses and insecurities,
Which you used to stroke your own ego.

I was the object of your affection,
But not of your respect,
–and so sweet words gave way to snide remarks.

While late night pleasures,
Would drift into early morning regrets.

You consumed me,
–heart, mind, and soul.

Still giving to me the greatest passion that I've ever known.
It's so very hard to walk away from that.

How can you walk away from what makes you feel good,
–if even for a little?

You become hurt to the point where your feelings go numb
and you feel no more of the passion that once consumed you.

The one thing that you gave to me that no one else did,
You destroyed.

All on your own–
You took away your own happiness.

# Break down

Deliberate arguments,
Picking apart our relationship,
Craving for you just to speak up.

Tell me I'm wrong,
And that you don't believe all of the things that I'm saying.

Open up your mouth,
And let dormant words of comfort and security flow freely,
Restoring my trust and putting me at ease.

Tell me that no matter how much I push you away,
You'll keep holding on tight as if it were for your life.

Set aside your pride,
And open up to me in ways that you've never opened up to
anyone before.

Give me one last chance before we call it quits for the
millionth time,
And then once finished–
Find a way to forgive me again, and never ever tell me that
we're done.

Please–

Show me that you care for me in more ways than one.

## Ramblings

Now playing: Isadora [Christian Scott]

What is love?

But a four letter word for the lovers who choose to indulge.

Crimson lips that stain collars—
Scarlett dresses, and late night gatherings that end with warm bodies under sweaty sheets.

Quick stops to the floral shop,
—and soft knocks on wooden red doors asking to come in.

Sultry looks that are always met with compliance,
—as fingertips graze over shoulders,
And voices drift to an inaudible tone.

Intellectual conversations about humanity, as you dive into each other's gentle but concentrated glances.

Quiet walks—
where the only exchange is ethereal.

Honest transparency of oneself,
Completely and genuinely.

Deep vibrational connections.

Transforming with its healing powers,
–yet asking for nothing in return.

It is the sweet soft melody that can be heard early in the morning as the birds sing.

Oh, love.
What is love?

# Love

I can't remember what real true love feels like–

What it actually is,
Is it rough around the edges?
Is it smooth like silk?

Does it fight?
Does it sit in silence, in a stance for peace?

Does it call late at night?
Or is it understanding that the other needs rest?

Is love reaching out gently to touch the others shoulder when
the other could care less?

Or is love leaving when you've had enough?

Is love patient?
Is it really kind?
Does it overlook shortcomings?
Does it get stronger over time?

What is love?

## Never Be

You and I will never be over,
Because a piece of me lies deep within you,
–and a piece of you lies deep within me.

You permeate every part of me,
–even existing as a filament of my soul.

And although I want to release you–
I can't,
Because it's out of my control.

In the depths of our existence we crave one another,
–even when we don't want to,
We still pang for each other.

You may leave in theory,
Never to return in physical form again,
–but the truth of the matter is that the love that expends
between us,
Will be for an eternity,
It will never end.

Owls

True love descends on the heart like an owl swooping over its
prey.
Eyes locked,
attention steady.

Quickly,
–yet gracefully ready.

Consuming in whole,
Leaving no remains behind.

No signs of the battle.
No signs of the bloodshed.
–only satisfaction remains.

As the owl sits heavily impassioned,
Full of desire–
And so full of love.

Full of everything that once was,
–but will never be.

## Reincarnation

In another life we were soulmates maybe,
Moving across time and space to find one another,
–but now our brokenness has made us both addicts,
Under recover.

Needing each other,
Longing for the love that the other gives.

And try as we may,
We've already ended before we've even decided to try again–
Without even the option of us remaining friends.

Because we love too passionately and fiercely to allow for
another lover to enter into,
 What was once, us.

So if we love so strongly,
Why did we end–

Trust.

## Repeat

Who could've ever known that forever would only last for a moment in time?

Surely someone must've known that forever would only be a fleeting moment.

And that just as we are born only to die,
–so do we fall in love, only to fall back out again.

## For a While

The pain of a breakup is the shortness of breath that I feel
when I think of you.

It's the darkness that blankets every corner of my room.

It's the coldness that I feel without your body here next to
mine.

The pain is piercing,
–throbbing like a second heartbeat.
It dies,
And then aches itself back to life–
Over and over and over again.

It's a realization that you are alone,
And without a part of yourself that is somewhere out in the
world alone and missing you too,
–or that is out,
Finding healing in another's embrace.

For a while it's intense,
Yet becomes over time a numbing sensation to the realization
that the love that once was,
Will never be,
Although it was supposed to be,

–for a while.

## I Must Be

If I must be broken apart piece by piece—

Deconstructed at the core and scattered across the floor...

If I'm expected to burn slowly,
—kindled by the infliction of the loss of the ones that I gave my heart to...

If I must die eventually,
—unable to be immortal because I too am imperfect...

Let me burn intensely in their sight,
As they watch me walk across a room.

While I'm being deconstructed by their fingertips as they undress me slowly and carefully.

Then let me transition by their side swiftly,
—and peacefully.

Because if I must be,
—then at least let me be by the side of the one that I love.

## Made

If I was made in His image, then I was made for love.

I was made for humanity, to believe in the good despite seeing the worst.

If I were made to love, then I should be more forgiving, more understanding...

Less feeling sorry for others, and instead replaced with feelings of empathy.

Made in His image?
–His likeness, truly?

Oh, yes. I was built sturdy, and able to defeat giants,
–yet still humble enough to make peace with lions.

Created to build the unimaginable and to serve others even when I am treated less than.

Put together in the palm of His hand.
Molded and shaped like clay on a potter's wheel.

I was created with the deepest love and appreciation for all that I'd become.

Truly through Him, I was made.

## The Giver

Who will give to the giver?

Who will love them when they have nothing left to give?

Who will sacrifice for them, and nurture them back into the beautiful giver that they once were,
before they gave every single thing that they had and became nothing?

Who will be the giver to the givers, when the giver has given their all and has nothing left to give?

## Affirmation

You are my Sunshine on the darkest of days–

You are the sun that lets down it's light on me,
The flowers that gently release their love in notes of citrus,
honey, and early morning dew.

You are my greatest gift–
And having you in my life affirms the Creator's love for my
very existence,
Simply because–
He gave you to me.

## Blessing

I remember the day that I knew that I would love you.
I was one week late,
And so scared to anticipate–
The thought of loving and caring for someone other than myself.

I didn't have much in regards to material possession,
But to think of ever giving you up, I could not imagine.

You were me.
An extension of my love,
my passion, and all that was and is good within me.
And I promised myself that what you gave to me,
I would return to you–
Love.

You are my blessing from God,
My motivation for pushing forward.
My inspiration for trying.

God gave my life meaning when he enabled for me to conceive you,
And to carry you to term.

Healthy and full of life,

He entrusted me to care for you,
–to love you,
And to guide you in his light and in His love.

So be patient with me as I learn to be everything that you need,
And everything that I was meant to be as your mother.

And never forget that I love you always.

Even when it doesn't seem that way,
always remember that I am your mother.

## City Lights

Now playing: Dance cadaverous [Wayne Shorter]

City lights,
They come alive at night,
–like lightning across the skyline.

Twinkling like stars,
Illuminating the skyscrapers,
–as if they were an overzealous crowd of paparazzi
photographers.

And even with streets as quiet as a holy temple,
–the city was alive!

It calls me here from where I lie,
In the dead of silence in my dark room.

It beckons me with its shadows moving about,
As humming cars drive pass my open window.

And even as my tiresome mind drifts off slowly into a restless
slumber,
I am lulled by the hypnotising clickety-clacking of a train
passing through the night.

City life.

## Sounds of Morning

Now playing: - Bye Bye Blackbird [Miles Davis]

Every morning I woke up to the soft lulling of her raspy melodic jazz music.

The warm notes sifted through the air and into my course tangled cold sheets, –and made them feel as gentle as Egyptian cotton.

She would tap about above me,
Making such beautiful and rhythmic melodies.

Tap-ety-tap–
Tic-ity-tap-tap...

Ooooh how she'd take me to far off continents with her myriad of music genres blaring from her window,
–as the strong fragrance of Columbian coffee seeped from her apartment and down to mine.

I'd sometimes see her out and about at the marketplace.
She'd be wearing the brightest most colorful ensemble of this and that,
–and the other of course.

She was just peculiar like that.

Otherworldly-like and ethereal,

–her voice as calming as the sound of birds singing beside my window.

Her spirit,

As vibrant as the myriad of colors that came through my window with the rising early morning sun.

She was the sound of morning.

## My HeArt

Sometimes I fall so deep into the imagery of art that I forget what made me truly fall in love with it.

—it's the ever evolving of the brush to the canvas...

It's that real art is never completed,
—each piece is a succession of the next,
It's a timeline of love, pain, and forgiveness.

It's passion and anger blended into beautiful hues that conspire to have us believe that it is one cohesive thought.

I love art because it is an escape from reality and social conformity,
—it doesn't require for me to define myself because I am granted the opportunity to love all of it.

Every
Single
Piece

—each one brings me a peace that can never be fully described in human words.

It's liberating and settling all at once,

Reminding me of just why I fell in love with these abstract
and surreal painted lines and shapes...

And that is because honestly and truly–
Art fell in love with me.

## Kinky

A kink, a curl, a coil,
God knows to my crown I've never been loyal.

From an early age I feigned for the creamy tonic that promised
to smooth my "nappiness" and turn it into soft manageable
happiness.

I bought the lie,
and then I purchased it again and again every six to eight
weeks.

I burned my scalp profusely,
wanting to be sure that every kink, curl, and coil was
obliterated.

I sang the catchy songs that came on the TV, after all this was
made just for me.

Made to tame my blackness,
And to mute my wild mane, all in the name of society's
definition of beauty.

It wasn't until I saw another woman,
with warm brown skin like mine–

And hair like wool, that I realized how beautiful I could be in my blackness.

Standing tall with an immense crown of kinky and untamed hair, she wasn't just beautiful,
–she was proud.

As she Walked passed strangers leaving a familiar scent of tropically sweet coconuts, fresh exotic fruits, and fragrant flowers–
With skin glistening from a blend of the sun's rays and silky raw shea butter.

She was an embodiment of all of the things that my soul desired to be, but had not the courage to embrace.

–until now.

## Afro-Dite

She lets her hair grow free, as wild and untamed as God created It.

And the coils in her hair between her thighs and either side of her heart grow just as kindly and unkempt as on her crown.

Her dark coils sit high, defying gravity and staying perfectly arranged like a sculpted topiary garden.

Everything on her body came directly from the almighty perfectly created. Nothing borrowed, nothing stolen, or emulated.

She is black gold.
Richly mahogany and opulently ebony.
She is a black woman in her unfiltered, unbothered, and unchained form.

She is free from the social and mental constraints of society...

Physically.
Mentally.
Spiritually.
She is free.

## Black Woman

Beautiful, black woman.
You are my muse. I draw my inspiration from you.

From your thick coarse hair that defies gravity, to your warm chocolate skin tone.

When I see you, something inside of me feels proud to be me. And proud to have such a rich heritage that is rooted so deeply and irrevocably into every single part of me.

Your strength encourages me.
It uplifts me.
It enlightens me.
And for that, I thank you.

Ebonics

I told you already, but I guess I'll hav'ta tell you again,

I didn't expand these hips and grow these heavy thighs for you.

I didn't let down my hair for your stares,

And I didn't wear this form fittin' dress to impress.

My beautifully adorned body
–from my pierced ears, to my studded nose, and all the way down to my painted toes–
was modified and emblazoned per my own specifications.

So nevermind your expectations.

Because I've always been too wild
Too loud
Too outspoken
Too thick
Too thin
Too in
Too out
Too much for those who never wanted me to begin with.

For those who fidget in their britches as they see me walk pass
–I hold my head a bit higher, and just look and laugh.

I notice the look in their eyes when they widen with curiosity
and surprise
–when they see my gravity defying hair and my full lips, and
taut skin.

Curiosity; then contempt.

For all of the things that they just cain't relate.
They'd rather I'd just –assimilate.

As they marinate in their ethnocentric haze, I just pour out
my love in infinite ways.

I keep pushin' forward, and I keep on bein' just what the good
Lord created me to be,
–me.

Although this is considered the end of this book, it will never truly be the end. As humans we continue to grow even in the absence of eyes that judge to tell us that we are moving too fast or too slow on our journey. The truth is that even in death, we will never cease to exist. We will only transfer as energy. This is also true of our time here on Earth. We will shift from old spaces and places into new spaces and places as we learn new lessons and evolve into better versions of ourselves. If you have made it to this page, I hope that something within these pages has resonated with you and has helped you to draw closer to yourself and to the beauty that lies within you.

Never forget that it is pain that gives birth to strength and resilience. It is pain that teaches the lesson and that urges us to find a new way to push forward and to not only survive, but to thrive. It is my prayer that you never ever give up, as there will *always* be new hope to be found in every lesson whether the lesson be painful or beautiful.

# ABOUT THE AUTHOR

Eve is a writer, mother, and dreamer who was born and raised in Detroit, MI among the sounds and soulful vibrations of Motown and the grit and hustle of urban city life.

When she isn't writing or spending time with her daughter, she can be found in the kitchen cooking while vibing out to some feel-good music. She is a lover of all things art and food related, and enjoys absorbing all of the healing essences of nature.

Eve is a firm believer in being intentional and being in tune with all of the parts of who she is and who she is evolving to be on her journey to self-love and living with less expectations, more gratitude, and more compassion. She hopes that while reading this book you will be inspired to reflect and to search within yourself to find the edification that you are seeking in your own life's journey.

*May all things good and lovely flow to you from now until eternity.*

*-Eve*